Robert Charles Winthrop

Oration on the 250th Anniversary of the Landing of the

Pilgrim Fathers at Plymouth

Robert Charles Winthrop

Oration on the 250th Anniversary of the Landing of the Pilgrim Fathers at Plymouth

ISBN/EAN: 9783337293321

Printed in Europe, USA, Canada, Australia, Japan

Cover: Foto ©Lupo / pixelio.de

More available books at **www.hansebooks.com**

ORATION

ON THE

Two Hundred and Fiftieth Anniversary

OF THE

LANDING

OF THE

PILGRIM FATHERS AT PLYMOUTH.

21 December, 1870.

BY

HON. ROBERT C. WINTHROP, LL.D.,

PRESIDENT OF THE MASSACHUSETTS HISTORICAL SOCIETY.

BOSTON:

PRESS OF JOHN WILSON AND SON.

1871.

THERE can be no true New England heart which does not throb to-day with something of unwonted exultation. There can be no true American heart, I think, which has not found itself swelling with a more fervent gratitude to God, and a more profound veneration for the Pilgrim Fathers, as this morning's sun has risen above the hill-tops, in an almost midsummer glory, and ushered in, once more, with such transcendent splendor, our consecrated Jubilee.

When we reflect on the influence which has flowed, and is still flowing, in ever fresh and ceaseless streams, from yonder Rock, which two centuries and a half ago was struck for the first time by the foot of civilized, Christian man; when we reflect how mightily that influence has prevailed, and how widely it has pervaded the world, — inspiring and aiding the settlement of Massachusetts, and, through Massachusetts, of all New England, and, through New England, of so large a part of our whole widespread country, and thus, through the example of

our country and its institutions, extending the principles of civil and religious freedom to the remotest
regions of the earth, leaving no corner of Christendom, or even of Heathendom, unvisited or unre-
freshed, — we should be dead, indeed, to every
emotion of gratitude to God or man, were we not
to hail this Anniversary as one of the grandest in
the calendar of the ages.

We are here, my friends, to celebrate the Fifth
Jubilee of what is now known emphatically, wherever the history of New England, or the history of
America, is read, as " The Landing." No other
landing, temporary or permanent, upon our own or
upon any other shore, can ever usurp its title, or ever
supersede or weaken its hold upon the world's
remembrance and regard.

There have been other landings, I need hardly
say, which have left a proud and shining mark on
the historic page: Landings of discoverers; landings of conquerors; landings of kings or princes,
called by right of restoration or revolution to take
possession of time-honored thrones ; landings of
organized Colonies, from large and well-appointed
fleets, on conspicuous coasts, to occupy territories
opened and prepared, in some degree, for human
habitation.

Not such was the landing which we commemorate to-day. Not such the event which has rendered this shortest day of all the year so memorable

for ever in the annals of human freedom. It was the landing of a few weary and wave-worn men from a single ship, — nay, from a single shallop, — on a bleak and desolate shore, amid the storms and tempests of a well-nigh arctic winter, with none to welcome, none even to witness it. I might, indeed, be almost pardoned for saying, that the sun itself stood still in the heavens to behold it! But there were, certainly, no other witnesses, save those witnesses to each other's constancy and courage who were themselves the actors in the scene, and that all-seeing, omnipresent God, who guided and guarded all their steps.

Turn back with me to that epoch of the winter solstice, just two hundred and fifty years ago, and let us spend at least a portion of this flying hour in attempting to recall the precise incidents which then occurred on the spot on which we are assembled, with some of their immediate antecedents and consequences. There have been, and will be, other occasions for boasting, if any one desires to boast, of what New England has accomplished, directly or indirectly, for herself or for mankind, in later times. There have been, and will be, other opportunities for a general glorification of New England principles, New England achievements, New England inventions and discoveries, past or present, remote or recent. We recognize them all to-day, — all, at least, that are worthy of being recognized at all, — as the legitimate result and development of this day's doings. We count and claim the progress of our country, in its best and worthiest sense, as the " Pilgrims' Progress; " — as the grand and glorious advance upon a line of march in which they were the pioneers, and for which they, in their own expressive phrase, literally as well as metaphorically, were the instruments " to break the ice for others."

To them the honors of this day are due. To their memories this Anniversary is sacred. Once in fifty years, certainly, we may well refresh our remembrance of what they did and suffered, and still more of the aims and ends of all their doings and sufferings. It is an old story, it is true; but there are some old stories which are almost forgotten into newness. There are some old stories which are actually new to every rising generation, and of whose real interest and nobleness thousands of young hearts receive their first vivid impression from what may be said or done on some occasion like the present. There are some old stories, too, of which even those who hold them in fondest and most familiar remembrance are never weary; and the appetite for which no repetitions can ever cloy, or even satisfy. There are some old stories, let me add, — and this is eminently one of them, — around which a haze, or it may be a halo, of legend and romance is gradually allowed to gather and thicken with the lapse of years, and which require and demand to be set forth afresh, from time to time, in their true simplicity and grandeur.

But there is no longer an excuse for doubt or uncertainty as to any substantial statement relating to the Pilgrim Fathers. Tradition, legend, romance, can find "no jutty, frieze, buttress, nor coigne of vantage, for their pendent bed and procreant cradle," in that solid structure of fact and truth which has recently been built up, — let me rather say, which has recently been discovered and unveiled, in all the simple beauty of its original proportions, — by the loving students and diligent investigators of Pilgrim history.

It is, indeed, a peculiar advantage of all young countries like our own, that, originating in a period of written and printed records, they may trace back the current of their career to its primal source and spring, without leaving room for any intermixture of myth or fable. Yet written or even printed records may disappear, or be overlooked and forgotten for a time, — awaiting such a search and such a scrutiny as Grote and Niebuhr, and Merivale and Mommsen, have recently brought to the history of Greece or Rome ; or as Froude, even more remarkably, has just given to the history of England's Queen Elizabeth.

Even such a search and such a scrutiny have of late been applied to the history of the little band

whose landing we are here to commemorate, and
most richly have they been rewarded. Since the
last Jubilee of the Pilgrims was celebrated, fifty
years ago, — when that grand discourse of New
England's grandest orator and statesman summoned
the attention of the world so emphatically to their
sublime but simple story, — antiquarians at home and
abroad, pious and painstaking students, American
travellers in foreign lands not forgetful of their own,
one and all, have seemed inflamed with a new zeal
to subject that story to the closest examination; to
sift out from it every thing conjectural and legendary;
and to investigate the Pilgrim track, footstep by
footstep, wherever it could be found, in the Old
World as well as in the New. Nothing has been
too minute or trivial to elude their search; nothing
too seemingly inscrutable to repel or discourage
their pursuit; nothing too generally credited to satisfy their eagerness for positive proof and authentic
verification. As the marvellous growth of that majestic perennial, of which the Mayflower supplied
the seed, has been developed and displayed, with
all its myriad leaves for the healing of the nations,
and all its magic branches for sweetening so many
bitter fountains, and all its rich and varied fruits for
ourselves and for mankind, they have been more and
more incited to trace back that seed to its native
bed; to analyze with almost chemical exactness its
smallest seminal principles; and to ascertain pre-

cisely by what culture, and by what hands, it was made so to take root upon a rock, and to bud and blossom and bear so abundantly in a wilderness.

We owe these laborious investigators a deep debt of gratitude, and it is fit that we should not forget them, this day, as we avail ourselves of their researches. I need but name the late admirable Judge Davis, whose excellent edition of "Morton's Memorial" led the way in the later illustrations of Pilgrim history. I need but name the late Reverend Dr. Alexander Young, whose "Chronicles of Plymouth" ought to be fresh in the memory of every son and daughter of the old Colony. But let me recall more deliberately a venerable antiquary of Old England, whom it was my good fortune to meet at the breakfast-table of the celebrated historian Hallam, nearly a quarter of a century ago, — the late Reverend Joseph Hunter; who, having diversified his routine of service, in her Majesty's Public Record Office, by tracts illustrative of the great triumphs of his own country in arms and in literature, — triumphs by the sword of Henry V. at Agincourt, and triumphs by the pens of Shakspeare and Milton in the fields of epic or dramatic poetry, — turned to the Pilgrims of Plymouth, and to the Puritans of Massachusetts, for the latest and best themes of his unwearied investigations. To him we primarily owe it that we can follow back that little band, to which the name of Brownists had been contemptuously given, to the very hive from which they first swarmed, — that little circle in Yorkshire and Nottinghamshire, and not far from Lincolnshire, around which he so fitly inscribed the legend, "Maximæ gentis incunabula," — the cradle of the greatest nation. By the light of his antiquarian torch we are able to fix the precise locality and surroundings of the old Manor Place of Scrooby, — formerly a palace of the Archbishops of York,. and which had often been the residence of at least one of them, "that he might enjoy the diversion of hunting" in the neighboring chase of Hatfield; which was occupied as a refuge for many weeks by the great lord Cardinal Wolsey, when, having "ventured in a sea of glory, but far beyond his depth," he had at last been left, "weary and old with service, to the mercy of a rude stream," which was for ever to hide him; and which, not many years afterwards, Henry the Eighth himself had selected for a resting-place, during one of his Royal progresses to the north; — but which, half a century later, had become the home of one, whose occupation of it, even for an hour, would have given it a celebrity and a sanctity in our remembrance and regard, which neither Archbishops, nor Cardinals, nor Kings, could have imparted to it in a lifetime.

There, in that "manor of the Bishops," of which, alas! hardly a fragment is now left, lived WILLIAM BREWSTER, — one of the noblest of the men whom we are here to commemorate, and not unworthy to be named first of all, on such an occasion as this. Educated at the University of Cambridge, and having served as the faithful Secretary of the accomplished Davison (Queen Elizabeth's Ambassador in Holland, and afterwards one of her Secretaries of State), — until Davison's too prompt and implicit obedience to the orders of his Royal Mistress in the matter of poor Mary, Queen of Scots, had afforded a pretext for discarding him, — Brewster had retired with disgust from the pomps and vanities, the caprices and cruelties, of the Court, and had given himself up to religious meditation and study. Deeply impressed with the corruptions and superstitions, the prelatical assumptions and tyrannies, of the English Church, as it then existed, in those earlier transition stages of the Reformation, he had united himself with one of the little bodies of Separatists from that communion, and soon became " a special help and stay to them." At his house, — this very "manor of the Bishops," which Mr. Hunter helped us to identify, — we learn that the members of the church of which the sainted Robinson was the pastor, the church of our Plymouth Pilgrims, "ordinarily met on the Lord's Day; and with great love he entertained them when they came, making provision for them to his great charge; and continued so to do while they could stay in England."

Our mother country has many spots within her

dominions which are dear to the hearts of the lovers of religious and of civil liberty in both hemispheres: The plain of Runnymede, the Lollard's Tower, the Tower of London, the Martyrs' Monument at Oxford, the glorious Abbey of Westminster, the grand Cathedrals in almost every county; but I know of none more worthy of being visited with pious reverence, by every American traveller certainly, than that old original site of Brewster's residence in Nottinghamshire; nor one which more deserves to be marked, not indeed by any ostentatious or sumptuous structure, out of all keeping with the plain and frugal character of those who have made it memorable for ever, but by some appropriate monument, a chapel or a school-house, erected by the care and at the cost of the sons and daughters of New England. We all remember that John Cotton's chapel at Old Boston was restored, not many years ago, by the contributions of a few of the generous sons of New Boston. The place where Robinson and Brewster gathered that first Pilgrim Church is certainly not less worthy of commemoration.

But it is not only the residence of Brewster which the researches of good Mr. Hunter, the very Nimrod of Antiquaries, have revealed to us. There, within that charmed circle — the cradle of the greatest nation — he helped us to discover a birthplace, which owing to a blundering misprint had so long baffled the most eager search; the birthplace of one who might almost contest with Brewster himself the right to be named first at any commemoration of the Pilgrim Fathers, — their Governor for thirty years, their Historian, their principal writer both in prose and verse, and second to no one of them, from first to last, in the fidelity and devotion with which he sustained and illustrated their principles. There, within that same charmed circle, of which the little market town of Bawtry is the centre, and the greater part, if not the whole, of which is now the property of one whose recent title, as a peer, has not obliterated our remembrance of his name as a poet, and who may be recalled with the more pleasure at this hour as one of the few among the English nobility who sympathized with the North in our late war for the Union, — there, in the record book of the little church of Austerfield, still standing, has been found the distinct entry, " William, son of William, Bradfourth, baptized the XIX.th day of March, Anno Dñi 1589."

I hold in my hand a photographic picture of that ancient edifice, and one, too, of the registered entry of Bradford's baptism, given me two or three years ago by Lord Houghton, — Monckton Milnes that was, — now Lord of the Manor, I believe, — and which I would gladly deposit in your Pilgrim Museum, if they are not there already.

The font from which Bradford was christened, and the altar-rails at which his parents doubtless kneeled — for he must have been baptized according to the rites, and by a pastor of the Church of England — are still preserved. But neither pastor nor parents could have dreamed, as the infant boy winced, perhaps, from the coldness of that sprinkled water, and shrunk, it may be, from the signing with the sign of the cross upon his tiny forehead, how sturdy and uncompromising a hater he was to become, in his mature life, of all mere forms and shows and ceremonies of religion; and, at the same time, how earnest and ardent and devoted a lover and upholder of the great truths and doctrines of which these were but the outward and visible signs.

Bradford and Brewster, if I mistake not, are the only two of our Pilgrim leaders, who can be distinctly identified with that little church at Scrooby, of which the venerable Richard Clifton and the zealous John Robinson were the associated pastor and teacher, and out of which came this first permanent settlement of New England. Bradford, indeed, was but a boy in age, at that early period, — hardly more than sixteen years old, an orphan boy, — and must have been like a son to Brewster, who was thirty years his senior; but he was a boy who seems to have known "little more of the state of childhood but its innocency and pleasantness," and who was capable, even then, of rendering no feeble aid and comfort to his maturer leader and friend. Together they braved persecution. Together they bore the taunts and scoffs of neighbors and relatives. Together they embraced exile. Together they were cast into prison at old Boston in Lincolnshire. Together, after a brief separation, — for Bradford was liberated first on account of his youth, — they found refuge in Holland. Together they embarked in the Mayflower. Together they were associated for three and twenty years, — for Brewster lived in a vigorous old age till 1643, — in establishing and ruling the Pilgrim plantation here at New Plymouth.

Brewster and Bradford, the Æneas and Ascanius of our grand Pilgrim Epic, — I might better have said, the Paul and Timothy, or be it Titus, of our New England, Plymouth, Separatist Church, — both of them laymen, but both of them, by life and word, by precept and example, showing forth the great doctrines of Christ, their Saviour, with a power and a persuasiveness which might well have been envied by any pastor or preacher or lordly prelate of that or any other day: — For ever honored be their names in New England history and in New England hearts! Alas! that no portrait of either of them is left, — if, indeed, in their simplicity and modesty, they would ever have allowed one to be taken, — so that their image, as well as their names and their example, might be held up to the contemplation of our country and of mankind for endless generations!

But the little church of which they were members was able, as we know, to maintain its precarious and perilous existence at Scrooby, for hardly more than a single year, certainly for not more than two years. It could find indeed no safe refuge or resting-place in Old England; and having heard that in the Low Countries, as they were then called, there was freedom, or at least toleration, for differences of religious faiths and forms, its members resolved to fly from persecution and establish themselves in Holland. I will not attempt to describe the perils they encountered, and the sufferings they endured, in that flight; — the separations of children from parents, and of wives from husbands; the arrests and examinations, the fines and imprisonments, to which so many of them were subjected; the "hair-breadth 'scapes" of one large party of them during a tempestuous voyage of fourteen days, in crossing the German Ocean, in an almost sinking ship. The whole story is familiar to you. It is enough that we find them all at last safely in Amsterdam, where they are free to enjoy their pure and simple worship, and where they remain quietly for another year.

Not a trace is left of their residence in that then mighty mart, almost a second Venice; born of the sea, "built in the very lap of the floods, and encircled in their watery arms;" and claiming the whole ocean, from the Baltic to the Levant, not only as the

field of its enterprise, but almost as its own rightful inheritance and domain. Not. a trace of them
is left there. We only know that, finding they
were in danger of being involved in contentions
about women's dresses and men's starched bands,
and other such vital matters, which had sprung up
in another little church of English Separatists which
had fled there before them, and thus of being robbed
of that harmony and peace which they prized above
all earthly things, and which they had abandoned
home and kindred and country to enjoy, — they
thought it best to remove once more, and establish
themselves at the neighboring inland city of Leyden.

It was a great epoch in Dutch history, when
the Pilgrims took up their abode in Holland, and
began to habituate themselves to its "strange and
uncouth" customs and language. It was the precise
period at which, as the close and consummation of
"the most tremendous war for liberty ever waged,"
our own Motley has terminated his admirable account of "The United Netherlands," — to begin it
again, we trust, at no distant day, and then to show
us precisely what was going on in that interesting country while our Fathers were witnesses and
partakers of its fortunes. Within a year after
they reached Amsterdam, and the very year they
removed to Leyden, the grand twelve years' truce
between Spain and her revolted Colonies had been
negotiated and ratified. Those Colonies had now

virtually established their freedom and independence. Olden Barneveldt and Prince Maurice had
reconciled their animosities and rivalries for a time;
and the great Republic — henceforth, though not
for ever, to be known and recognized as the United
States of the Netherlands — was enjoying internal
as well as external peace and rest, after a fearful
struggle of forty years' duration.

It is a charming coincidence, certainly, that the
coming of the Pilgrims was thus simultaneous with
the commencement of that blessed truce, which
was destined, too, by its own limitation, to last during the precise period of their stay there. One
might almost picture the bow of peace and promise,
lifting itself in all its many-colored glories, and over-
arching that blood-stained soil, to welcome the little
band of fugitives for conscience' sake to their temporary repose, and to assure them that war should
crimson its fields no more while they should bless
it with their presence!

At Leyden, they find, as Bradford says, "a fair
and beautiful city, and of a sweet situation, but made
more famous by the University wherewith it is
adorned, in which of late had been so many learned
men." That was, certainly, a noble University,
erected as a monument to the heroism of those who
had fought and fallen in the dreadful siege which
the city had endured so grandly in 1574, — erected
in the same spirit in which our Memorial Hall has

recently been founded at Cambridge by the Alumni
of Harvard. Famous professors, and famous schol-
ars also, it had indeed enjoyed. The learned
Arminius had died just as the Pilgrims arrived
there, but his teachings and doctrines were left to
be the subject of endless disputation. The marvellous Joseph Scaliger, too, had died the same year;
but his not less marvellous pupil, Hugo Grotius,
was only at the outset of his great career, having
published his Latin Tragedy, " The Suffering
Christ," the very year of their arrival at Amsterdam, and his " Mare Liberum " the year of their
removal to Leyden.

The youthful Bradford may not, perhaps, have
been much in the way of taking note or notice of
what was going on at this great seat of learning,
as, in default of other means of support, he had put
himself as an apprentice to a French Protestant,
and was acquiring the art of dyeing silk. But Brewster had found employment as a tutor to some of the
youth of the city and the University, and was teaching them the English language by a grammar of his
own construction; while, at the same time, he had set
up a printing-press, and " was instrumental in pub-
lishing several books against the hierarchy, which
could not obtain a license in England." To him the
University and its learned professors, and all their
proceedings and lectures, must have been as familiar as they were interesting. His revered friend

and pastor, Robinson, moreover, — as we learn from the researches of an accomplished and lamented New England scholar and traveller (the late Mr. George Sumner), — was formally admitted to the privileges of a member or subject of the University four or five years after his arrival at Leyden. By the investigations of Mr. Sumner, too, and of a late American Minister at the Hague, the Hon. Henry C. Murphy, we have been enabled to identify the very spot, in the Cathedral Church of St. Peter, where the precious remains of this holy man, whose memory is so dear to New England, were at least temporarily deposited; while the record of that burial has also most happily helped us to fix the exact place of his residence as long as he lived there. In that residence, — and not in any church edifice, for they had none, — there is the best reason for thinking that the Pilgrims worshipped; and thanks to the pious pains of the Rev. Henry Martyn Dexter, of Boston, whose labors in the cause of Pilgrim history I may find further cause for acknowledging, a plate has been affixed to the walls of the building which now stands on that site, inscribed, "On this spot lived, taught and died, JOHN ROBINSON, 1611–1625."

I cannot forget that I lingered in Leyden, for some hours, two or three years ago, for the single purpose of visiting that site, and the place of the grave of him who made it so memorable for ever;

but I could find no one at hand to point either of them out for me; and, but for the record of Mr. Sumner and the inscription of Dr. Dexter, I might have missed all that there is there to recall the memory of the Fathers of New England. For, indeed, this is all, — the place of a temporary grave and the site of a dwelling long ago levelled to the ground, — this is absolutely all which can be identified of the Pilgrims' home at Leyden for eleven years. Yet no New Englander, I think, can visit that city on an early autumn or a late summer's day, and behold the ancient buildings on which their eyes must have been accustomed to look; and gaze on the countless canals, and on the flowing river, on the bosom of which they must so often have sailed, and on the banks of which they must so often have rested ; and drink in that soft, hazy, golden sunshine, which one of the great masters of that region (Cuyp), not far from the very time and place at which they were enjoying it, was engaged in making the chief charm of not a few of his most exquisite landscapes, — without being conscious of the inspiration of the scene; nor without feeling and acknowledging that there is, and will for ever be, a magnetic sympathy between Leyden and Plymouth Rock, which no material batteries or tangible wires are needed to kindle and keep alive.

Leyden must indeed have been, as we know it was, most dear to the hearts of the Pilgrim Fathers.

There they found rest and safety. There, to use their own language, they enjoyed " much sweet and delightful society and spiritual comfort together in the ways of God," and " lived together in peace and love and holiness." But there, too, they were joined by not a few of those who were to be most service-able and most dear to them in their future experi-ences and trials.

There they were joined by JOHN CARVER, of whom we know enough for his own glory, and for his perpetual remembrance among men, in know-ing almost nothing except that he was counted worthy to be chosen the first Governor of the little band, and that he died, here at Plymouth, after a brief career, in the faithful discharge of that office.

There ROBERT CUSHMAN joined them, who, in spite of some infirmities of temper and some infelic-ities of conduct, and though at one time he seemed to have "put his hand to the plough and to have looked back," and was missing from the group whose advent we celebrate to-day, came over not long afterwards, reinstated in the confidence of those with whom he had been so prominently asso-ciated at Leyden; delivered, in the Common House of the Plantation, that memorable sermon on Self-Love, the first printed sermon of New England, if not of our whole continent; and, after a perhaps pre-mature return home, continued to watch carefully over the interests of the Pilgrims in England, writing letters remarkable alike for the beauty of their style and for the prudence of their counsel; and was lamented by Bradford, when he heard of his death in 1624, as " a wise and faithful friend."

There they were joined by MILES STANDISH, the intrepid soldier and famous captain of New England; who, having served on the side of the Dutch in the armies of England in the war against Spain, and having now been released by the great truce from further campaigning in the Old World, united himself with the Pilgrims, and, though not a member of their church, followed their fortunes, and fought their battles gallantly to the end. A little man himself, — hardly more than five feet high, — the grand army with which he performed " his most capital exploit" was probably the smallest which was ever mustered for a serious conflict in the annals of human warfare, — only eight men besides their leader. But, " in small room large heart inclosed," he had acquired, not perhaps from Cæsar's Commentaries, his favorite study, but certainly from some other source, a knowledge which some of the ruthless warriors of the present day have failed to exhibit, — the knowledge where to stop, as well as when to strike; and, having secured a signal victory, he brought home in safety every man whom he carried out. Honor to Miles Standish, " the stalwart captain of Plymouth," of whose restrained wrath, when the Puritan influence had come in to temper the profanity for which there was a proverbial license in Flanders, our charming Longfellow would seem to have caught the very accent and cadence, when he says of it, —

"Sometimes it seemed like a prayer, and sometimes it sounded like swearing;"

and whose threefold accomplishments he so tersely sums up, when he describes him as doubting

" Which of the three he should choose for his consolation and comfort,
Whether the wars of the Hebrews, the famous campaigns of the Romans,
Or the artillery practice, designed for belligerent Christians."

A higher tribute to the fidelity, vigilance, and courage of the old Plymouth captain could hardly have been paid, than when the late venerable Judge Davis, — a Plymouth man, and full of the original Plymouth spirit, — not many years before his death, unwilling to be wanting to the volunteer patrol service. in Boston, on some occasion of real or imaginary peril, made solemn application to our old Massachusetts Historical Society for the use of one of his reputed — albeit somewhat rusty — swords, and walked the midnight round with that for his trusty and all-sufficient companion.

But there, too, at Leyden, they were joined, — by the accidents of travel, as it would seem, — in 1617, by one of the very noblest of our little band, who was soon associated most leadingly and lovingly

with all their spiritual as well as temporal concerns;
their Governor for three years, when Bradford had
" by importunity got off;" the narrator and chron-
icler of not a few of the most interesting passages
of their history; the leader of not a few of their
most important enterprises; a man of eminent activ-
ity, resolution, and bravery; who did not shrink from
offering himself as a hostage to the savages, while
a conference was held and a treaty made with one
of their barbarous chieftains; who did not shrink
from imprisonment, and the danger of death, in con-
fronting, as an agent of Plymouth and Massachusetts,
the tyrannical Archbishop Laud; who earned a
gentler and more practical title to remembrance as
the importer of the first neat cattle ever introduced
into New England; an earnest and devoted friend
to the civilization of the Indian tribes and their conversion to Christianity; the chief commissioner of
Oliver Cromwell in his warlike designs upon an
island, which our own hero President has so recently
attempted to secure by peaceful purchase:—EDWARD
WINSLOW,—the only one of the Pilgrim Fathers of
whom we have an authentic portrait; whose old
seat of Careswell, at Marshfield, was the chosen
home of Webster; and whose remains, had they not
been committed to the deep, when he died so sadly
on the sea, at the close of his unsuccessful expedi-
tion to St. Domingo, would have been counted
among the most precious dust which New England
could possess. 4

Leyden must indeed have been dear to the Pilgrims, as the place where so many of these leading spirits first entered into their association, and first pledged their lives and fortunes to the sacred enterprise.

But Leyden, and the whole marvellous land of which it was at that day one of the most interesting and enlightened cities, had a charm for our Forefathers far above all mere personal considerations. It was a land to which the great German poet, dramatist, and historian, Schiller, in his " Revolt of the Netherlands," gave the noblest testimony, in saying that " every injury inflicted by a tyrant gave a right of citizenship in Holland." It was a land to which that quaint old Suffolk County essayist, Owen Felltham, paid a still higher tribute when he described it as "a place of refuge for sectaries of all denominations." " Let but some of our Separatists be asked," said he, with evident reference to our English exiles of whom he was a contemporary, " let but some of our Separatists be asked, and they shall swear that the Elysian Fields are there." " If you are unsettled," says he in another place, " if you are unsettled in your religion, you may try here all, and take at last what you like best. If you fancy none, you have a pattern to follow of two that would be a church by themselves."

Yes, that was exactly it, — "a Church by themselves;" and there, in that church by themselves,

our Pilgrim Fathers first tasted the sweets of civil
and religious freedom, and enjoyed that liberty to
worship God, according to the dictates of their
own consciences, which to them was worth every
sacrifice and above all price. There, too, just
as they removed from Amsterdam to Leyden, the
extraordinary sound was heard, — from the lips
of a Roman Catholic, and in behalf of his Roman
Catholic brethren, — of an appeal for liberty of
conscience which was never surpassed by the
founders of Rhode Island, Maryland, or Pennsylvania. "Those," said President Jeannin, most forcibly and eloquently, on taking leave of the States
General, "those cannot be said to share any enjoy-
ment from whom has been taken the power of serving God according to the religion in which they
were brought up. On the contrary, no slavery is
more intolerable nor more exasperates the mind
than such restraint. You know this well, my Lords
States; you know, too, that it was the principal,
the most puissant cause that made you fly to arms
and scorn all dangers, in order to effect your deliv-
erance from this servitude. You know that it has
excited similar movements in various parts of Christendom, and even in the kingdom of France, with
such fortunate success everywhere as to make it
appear that God had so willed it, in order to prove
that religion ought to be taught and inspired by the
movements which come from the Holy Ghost, and
not by the force of man."

We know not precisely how far the ears of the
Pilgrims may have been regaled, and their hearts
encouraged and strengthened, by this grand appeal
from so unaccustomed a source. Brewster, who,
as we have seen, had been in the Low Countries
before, as Secretary to the English Ambassador,
may hardly have been ignorant of it. But, at all
events, it affords most significant testimony to the
spirit of religious liberty which pervaded the land
in which such words at that period could have been
uttered; and, coming from the lips of a Romanist, it
must have put to shame any Protestant bigotry or
intolerance, if any such were lurking there, which
might have restrained the full freedom of our English exiles. Dr. Belknap, in his American Biogra-
phy, may, perhaps, have anticipated events in stating,
as he does, that Robinson himself, about this time,
after a friendly conference with one upon whose name
he had recently made a petulant pun, in an angry
controversy, — changing it reproachfully from Ames
to *Amiss*, — relaxed the rigor of his Separatism;
published a book, allowing and defending the lawfulness of communicating with the Church of England;
" allowed pious members of the Church of England,
and of all the reformed churches, to communicate
with his church; and declared that he separated
from no church, but from the corruptions of all
churches." But the statement was substantially
true of a later period, if not of this. The book, he

adds, gained him the title of a Semi-Separatist, and was so offensive to the rigid Brownists of Amsterdam that they would scarcely hold communion with the Church of Leyden.

But, alas! more serious dissensions than these were soon to agitate again that whole united Republic, and to involve it in a crime of which all the multitudinous seas which surround it could hardly wash out the stain. The successor to the chair of Arminius in the University of Leyden (Vorstius) had not only stirred up "hearts of controversy" in his own land by teaching and preaching the peculiar doctrines of his master, but had roused the special indignation of the Royal theological polemic and titular Defender of the Faith across the channel, — that same James I., who a few years before had cut short a conference with the Puritan leaders, at Hampton Court, by declaring that "he would make them conform or he would harry them out of the land," and who, in this respect certainly, had been as good as his word. The recent assassination of his glorious fellow-sovereign, Henry IV. of France, had revived and quickened his antipathy not to Roman Catholics only, but to all religionists who did not agree with himself; and he had the insolence now to demand that the obnoxious Professor of Leyden should be dismissed from his chair and banished from the States, — leaving it, also, to their "Christian wisdom" whether he should not be

burned at the stake for "his atheism and blasphe-
mies." The States were compelled to comply, and
did most humiliatingly comply, with this demand;
but the banishment of Vorstius only the more
inflamed the theological strife which raged throughout their dominions. Prince Maurice and Olden
Barneveldt were again at each other's throats; the
former as the leader of the Calvinist party, and the
latter as the leader of the Arminians, with Grotius
as his second. And, incredible as it seems to us at
this hour, the controversy was only terminated by
one of the most infamous judicial murders which
pollute the annals of mankind; taking its loath-
some place in the calendar of crime by the side of
the execution of Sir Walter Raleigh, the year before,
and of Algernon Sydney and Lord William Russell
half a century later. On the 13th of May, 1619,
Olden Barneveldt, the noble patriot and benefactor,
second to no one among the founders of the Republic and the authors of its liberties, was condemned
to death and beheaded at the Hague; while Grotius
was sentenced to perpetual imprisonment, — from
which, however, the ingenuity of his wife happily
released him at the end of two years.

I would gladly have found some allusion to these
monstrous outrages in some of the journals or letters
of the Pilgrims. Occurring, as they did, during the
very last year of their residence there, I would
gladly believe that some abhorrence of such crimes

may have mingled with their motives for seeking another place of refuge. Although their religious sympathies were strongly with the Calvinist party, and their pastor, Robinson, had disputed publicly against the doctrines of Arminius, — putting his antagonist Episcopius, the Arminian Professor, to "an apparent nonplus," as Bradford tells us, "not once only, but a second and third time, before a great and public audience, and winning a famous victory for the truth," and "much honor and respect for those who loved the truth," — yet he and Brewster and Bradford and Winslow must have shrunk with horror from this atrocious murder. There is good reason for believing that Brewster, indeed, left Leyden with his family not many weeks afterwards; and I will not doubt that such events increased the eagerness of them all once more to change the place of their habitation, and hastened their negotiations with the merchant adventurers in London.

But their purpose of quitting Holland had been conceived nearly two years before this terrible tragedy was enacted. As early as the autumn of 1617, Robert Cushman and John Carver had been sent as their agents to attempt an arrangement for their removal to America with the Virginia Company in London; and in 1618 the Church of Leyden — with a view to removing the objections, and conciliating the favor of the King and others — had adopted those memorable Seven Articles, first published in 1856 by our accomplished historian Bancroft, in which the authority of his Majesty and of his Bishops is acknowledged, with an unqualified assent "to the confession of faith published in the name of the Church of England and to every article thereof." The adoption of these " Seven Articles," and the appeals addressed to Sir Edwin Sandys and others by Brewster and Robinson, at length elicited an assurance that "both the King and the Bishops had consented to wink at their departure."

" Conniving at them and winking at their departure " were all the assurances they could wring from Royalty. " To allow or tolerate them by his public authority, under his seal, they found it would not be." And though the Virginia Company were strongly desirous to have them go to America under their auspices, and willing to grant them a patent with as ample privileges as they could grant to any one, the feuds and factions in the council of the Company occasioned such delays that no patent was sealed until the 9th of June, 1619; and, after all the labor and cost of procuring it, it was never made use of. An agreement, however, was entered into with Thomas Weston and other merchant adventurers; the Mayflower was hired to await them at Southampton; the Speedwell was bought to take them over to England, and keep them company afterwards; a day of solemn humiliation was spent, — after a parting sermon from Robinson, who was to remain behind with half the members of his church, — "in pouring out prayers to the Lord with great fervency mixed with abundance of tears," and so they proceeded to Delft Haven; and after another most touching parting scene, all kneeling in prayer and taking leave of each other, "with mutual embraces and many tears," the sail was hoisted, and with a prosperous wind they came in a short time to Southampton. There they found "the bigger ship come from London, lying ready, with all the rest of their company." A few days more are occupied in dealing with their agents and the merchant adventurers; a noble farewell letter from Robinson is received and read; and once more they set sail. A leak in the Speedwell compels them to put in at Dartmouth, and then again, after they had gone above a hundred leagues beyond Land's End, to put back to Plymouth, and to abandon the Speedwell altogether. At last, "these troubles being blown over, and now all being compact together in one ship, they put to sea again with a prosperous wind;" and on the 16th day of September, 1620, Old England is parted from for ever. The Mayflower, and its one hundred and two passengers, have entered on the voyage, which is to end not merely in founding a more memorable Plymouth than that which they left behind, but in laying the corner-stone of a mightier and freer nation than the sun in its circuit had ever before shone upon.

England at the moment took no note of their departing. Her philosophers and statesmen and poets had not quite yet begun to appreciate the losses which religious persecution was entailing upon her. Lord Bacon, indeed, "the great Secretary of Nature and all learning," as Isaac Walton called him, had already foreshadowed the glory which was to be gained by some of his Suffolk and Lincolnshire neighbors, when, in one of his celebrated essays, he assigned the first place, "in the true marshalling of the degrees of sovereign honor," to the "*conditores imperiorum*,—the founders of States and Commonwealths." But it was more than ten years afterwards before the saintly Herbert published those noted lines, which the Vice-Chancellor of Cambridge had so much hesitation about licensing : —

> " Religion stands on tiptoe in our land,
> Readie to passe to the American strand."

And it was nearly ten years later still, when John Milton, in his treatise " Of Reformation in England," exclaimed, " What numbers of faithful and free-born Englishmen, and good Christians, have been constrained to forsake their dearest home, their friends and kindred, whom nothing but the wide ocean, and the savage deserts of America, could hide and shelter from the fury of the bishops! Oh, sir, if we could but see the shape of our dear mother England, as poets are wont to give a personal form to what they please, how would she appear, think ye, but in a mourning weed, with ashes upon her head, and tears abundantly flowing from her eyes, to behold so many of her children exposed at once, and thrust from things of dearest necessity, because their conscience could not assent to things which the bishops thought indifferent!"

But the time was to come when England was to make signal recognition of this memorable Exodus. Little did they imagine, — those pious, humble, simple-hearted men and women, as they stood on the deck of their little bark of only one hundred and eighty tons' burthen, and looked wistfully upon their native shores receding from their moistened eyes, — little did they imagine that the scene of that embarkation, before two centuries and a half had passed away, should not only be among the most cherished ornaments of the Rotundo of the American Capitol, but should be found, as it is found this day, among the most conspicuous frescoes in the corridors of the Parliament Houses of Old England. Still less could the haughty Monarch and the bigoted Prelates, who had reluctantly been induced "to connive and wink at their departure," have dreamed, that such a picture should ever be warranted and welcomed by their successors, as one of the appropriate scenes for inspiring and for warning them, as they should sweep along, through the grand galleries of State, to their places on the throne or the Episcopal bench, in that gorgeous Chamber of the temporal and spiritual Lords of Great Britain.

But this would not be the only souvenir of the
Pilgrim Fathers which might suffuse the cheeks of
a Bancroft, a Wren, or a Laud, could they be permitted to revisit the scenes of their old prelatical
intolerance and arrogance.

The suburban residence of the Bishop of London
at Fulham has many charms. Its velvet lawn, its
walks upon the Thames, its grand old oaks and
cedars of Lebanon, its fine historical portraits, its
rare library, its beautiful modern chapel, and, above
all, its antique hall, recently restored, — in which the
cruel Bonner and the noble Ridley may have successively held their councils during the struggles of the
Reformation, and where Bancroft and Laud may have
concerted their schemes of bigotry and persecution,—
render it altogether one of the most interesting places
near London, and hardly less attractive than Lambeth
itself. I have been privileged to visit it on more
than one of those delicious afternoons of an English
June, when the apartments and the grounds were
thronged by all that was most distinguished in the
society of the Metropolis, assembled to pay their
respects to one whose exalted character, and earnest
piety, and liberal churchmanship, and unsparing
devotion to the humblest as well as the highest
duties of his station, have won for him universal
esteem, respect, and affection, and who has recently
been called by the Queen to the Primacy of all
England. But I need hardly say, that to an Ameri-

can, or certainly to a New England eye, there was nothing in all the treasures of art, or of antiquity, or of literature, which that palace contained, — nothing in all the loveliness of its natural scenery and surroundings, nothing in all the historical associations of the spot, nothing in all the beauty and accomplishments and titled or untitled celebrity of the company gathered beneath the roof or scattered upon the lawn, — which could compare for a moment with the interest of an old manuscript volume, which strangely enough had found its way there, of all places in the world, and which had rested for three quarters of a century almost unidentified and unrecognized on its library-shelves. You will all have anticipated me when I say that it is the long-lost manuscript volume, of which but a small portion had ever been printed or copied, written by the hand of William Bradford himself, and giving the detailed story of the Pilgrim Fathers from their first gathering at Scrooby down to the year 1647.

My valued friend, Mr. Charles Deane, to whom, above almost all others, we are indebted for throwing light upon the early history of New England, in the edition of this volume which he so admirably prepared and annotated for the Collections of the Massachusetts Historical Society, has sufficiently described the circumstances of its discovery. When the glad tidings first reached us, I did not fail to sympathize with those who felt that a more rightful as well as more congenial and appropriate place for such a manuscript might be found on this side of the Atlantic. But after a little more reflection, and after we had secured an exact and complete transcript of it for publication, I could not help feeling that there was something of special fitness and felicity in its being left precisely where it is. There let it rest, as a remembrancer to all who shall succeed, generation after generation, to that famous See and its charming palace, of the simple faith, the devoted piety, the brave obedience to the dictates of conscience, of those who led the way in the colonization of New England, and who endured so heroically the persecutions and perils which that great enterprise involved!

How it would have gratified the honest heart of Bradford himself, could he have known where his precious volume should at length be found, and in what estimation it should be held after it was found! How it would have delighted him to know that instead of being set down in some " Index Expurgatorius," or burned at St. Paul's Cross, as compounded of heresy and blasphemy, — as it would have been by those who dwelt or congregated at Fulham at the time it was written, — it should be sacredly guarded among the heirlooms of the palace and its successive occupants! How much more it would have delighted him to know that so much of the simplicity and liberality of form and faith which

it portrayed and inculcated, would be cherished and
exemplified by more than one of those under whose
official custody it was in these latter days to fall!

Few persons, I presume, will doubt that had the
Church of England, between 1608 and 1620, been
what it is to-day, and its Bishops and Archbishops
such in life and in spirit as those who have recently
presided at London and Canterbury, Brewster and
Bradford would hardly have left Scrooby, and the
Mayflower might long have been employed in less
interesting ways than in bringing Separatists to
Plymouth Rock. As that church and its prelates
then were, let us thank God that such Separatists
were found! An Episcopalian myself, by election
as well as by education, and warmly attached to the
forms and the faith in which I was brought up; believing that the Church of England has rendered inesti-
mable service to the cause of religion in furnishing
a safe and sure anchorage in so many stormy times,
when the minds of men were " tossed to and fro,
and carried about with every wind of doctrine;"
and prizing that very prayer-book, — which was dis-
owned and discarded by Bradford and Brewster,
and by Winthrop, too, — as second only to the Bible
in the richness of its treasures of prayer and praise;
I yet rejoice, as heartily as any Congregationalist
who listens to me, that our Pilgrim Fathers were
Separatists.

I rejoice, too, that the Puritan Fathers of Massachusetts, who followed them to these shores ten years afterwards, — though, to the last, they "esteemed it their honor to call the Church of England their dear mother, and could not part from their native country, where she specially resideth, without much sadness of heart and many tears," — were, if not technically and professedly, yet to all intents and purposes, Separatists, also; — Semi-Separatists at least, as Robinson himself was called when he wrote and published that book which so offended the Brownists. I rejoice that the prelatical assumptions and tyrannies of that day were resisted. The Church of England would never have been the noble church it has since become, had there been no seasonable protest against its corruptions, its extravagant formalism, and its overbearing intolerance. The earliest Separatists were those who separated from Rome; and when something more than a disposition was manifested to return towards Rome, in almost every thing except the acknowledgment of its temporal supremacy, another separation could not have been, ought not to have been, avoided. A serious renewal of such manifestations at this day, I need not say, would rend the Anglican Church asunder ; and its American daughter would, under similar circumstances, deservedly share its fate. Pretensions of human infallibility need not be proclaimed by an Ecumenical Council in order to be offensive and abhorrent. It does not require a conclave of Cardinals to render assumptions and proscriptions and excommunications odious. Convocations and Conventions, and even Synods and Councils and Conferences, will answer just as well. When so much of the discipline of the English Church was devoted to matters of form and ceremony; when spiritualism was in danger of forgetting its first syllable, and of degenerating into an empty ritualism; when godly ministers were silenced for "scrupling the vestments," or for preaching an evening lecture, and men and women and children were punished for not bowing in the Creed, or kneeling at the altar, or for having family prayers under their own roof, — separation — call it Schism, if you will — was the true resort and the only remedy. For the sake of the church itself, but a thousand-fold more for the sake of Christianity, which is above all churches, it was needful that a great example of such a separation should be exhibited at all hazards and at any sacrifice. The glorious Luther, to whose memory that majestic monument has so recently been erected at Worms, had furnished such an example in his own day and land, and with relation to the church of which he had once been a devoted disciple. No name may be compared with his name in the grand calendar of Separatists. But our Pilgrim Fathers were humble followers in the same path of Protestantism, and thanks be to God that their hearts were inspired and emboldened to imitate his heroic course.

I would not seem too harsh towards those old prelates of the English Church, by whom Pilgrims or Puritans were persecuted. Sir James Mackintosh, I think, has somewhere said, that if the United Netherlands had erected a statue to the real author of all their liberties, it would have been to the Duke of Alva, whose abominable tyranny goaded the Dutch to desperation, and drove them into rebellion. I am not sure that, on this principle, New England might not well include Bancroft and Laud in her gallery of eminent benefactors. We must never forget, however, that almost all great movements are but the resultants of opposing forces; and that, in impressing upon them their final shape and direction, those who resist are hardly less effective than those who support and urge. Nor can it be forgotten that, in the turn of the wheel of England's fortunes, poor Laud was himself destined to persecution and martyrdom. It must have been a grim joke, when Hugh Peters and others proposed to send him over to New England for punishment, as his Breviate tells us they did; and it might be a matter for curious conjecture what would have happened to him, had he come here then. But the meekness and bravery and Christian heroism with which he bore his fate, when so wantonly and barbarously brought to the block, after four years of imprisonment in the Tower, are almost enough to make us forget that he was ever so haughty and insolent and cruel, and quite enough to extinguish all resentment of his wrongs.

But let me not longer delay to acknowledge, on this occasion, the deep debt which New England and our whole country owes to the Congregationalism which the Pilgrims established on our soil, and of which the very first church in America was planted by them here at Plymouth. My whole heart is in sympathy with the celebration of this Jubilee to be held in my native city, this evening, by the Congregationalists of our land. They would wrong themselves, indeed, as well as all who are not of their own communion, were they to celebrate it in any narrow, controversial spirit, and to turn a national into a merely denominational anniversary. But it would be doing them deep injustice to suggest or imagine such a thing. They have a right to celebrate it, and they will celebrate it, as a day whose associations and influences have far outreached every thing sectarian and every thing sectional, and which are as comprehensive as the land they live in, and as all-embracing as the Christianity they profess and cherish.

Few persons, if any, can hesitate to agree with them, that no other system of church government than Congregationalism could have been successful in New England at that day. No other system

could have done so much for religion ; no other
system could have done so much for liberty, religious or civil. "The meeting-house, the school-
house, and the training field," said old John Adams,
"are the scenes where New England men were
formed." He did not intend to omit the town-
house, for no one was more sensible than himself
how much of New England education and character was owing to our little municipal organizations,
and to the free consultations and discussions of our
little town meetings. But he was right in naming
"the meeting-house" first. Certainly, for the cause
of religious freedom, no other security could have
compared with the independent system of church
government. Independent churches prepared the
way for Independent States and an Independent
Nation; and formed the earliest and most enduring
barriers and bulwarks at once against hierarchies
and monarchies.

That work fully and finally accomplished, and
civil and religious freedom securely established, we
may all be more than content, we all ought to
rejoice, as we witness the association and the prosperous advancement, under whatever name or form
they may choose to enroll themselves, of "all who
profess and call themselves Christians," — studying
ever, as Edward Winslow tells us the sainted
Robinson studied, towards his latter end, "peace
and union as far as might agree with faith and a

good conscience." Let those who will, indulge in the dream, or cherish the waking vision, of a single universal Church on earth, recognized and accepted of men, whose authority is binding on every conscience and decisive of every point of faith or form. To the eye of God, indeed, such a Church may be visible even now, in "the blessed company of all faithful people," in whatever region they may dwell, with whatever organization they may be connected, with Him as their head, "of whom the whole family in earth and heaven is named." And as, in some grand orchestra, hundreds of performers, each with his own instrument and his own separate score, strike widely variant notes, and produce sounds, sometimes in close succession and sometimes at lengthened intervals, which heard alone would seem to be wanting in every thing like method or melody, but which heard together are found delighting the ear, and ravishing the soul, with a flood of magnificent harmony, as they give concerted expression to the glowing conceptions of some mighty master, like him, the centennial anniversary of whose birthday has just been commemorated, — even so, — even so, it may be, — from the differing, broken, and often seemingly discordant strains of sincere seekers after God, the Divine ear, upon which no lisp of the voice or breathing of the heart is ever lost, catches only a combined and glorious anthem of prayer and praise!

But to human ears such harmonies are not vouch-safed. The Church, in all its majestic unity, shall be revealed hereafter. The "Jerusalem, which is the mother of us all, is above;" and we can only humbly hope that, in the providence of God, its gates shall be wider, and its courts fuller, and its members quickened and multiplied, by the very differences of form and of doctrine which have divided Christians from each other on earth, and which have created something of competition and rivalry, and even of contention, in their efforts to advance the ends of their respective denominations. Absolute religious uniformity, as poor human nature is now constituted, would but too certainly be the cause, if it were not itself the consequence, of absolute religious indiffer-ence and stagnation.

Pardon me, fellow-citizens and friends, for a digression, — if it be one, — in which I may almost seem to have forgotten that I have been privileged to occupy this pulpit only for a temporary and secular purpose, and to have encroached on the pre-rogative of its stated incumbent; but coming here, at your flattering call, to unite in the commemoration of those whose special distinction it was to have separated from the communion to which I rejoice to belong, I could not resist the impulse to give utterance to thoughts which are always uppermost in my mind, when I reflect on this period of New England history. I hasten now to resume and to finish the thread of that Pilgrim narrative which is the legitimate theme of my discourse.

I must not detain you for a moment by the details of that perilous voyage across the Atlantic, with its " many fierce storms, with which the ship was badly shaken and her upper works made very leaky; and one of the mainbeams in the midships bowed and cracked." I must not detain you by dwelling on that " serious consultation " in mid-ocean about putting back, when " the great iron screw which the passengers brought out of Holland " was so providentially found " for the buckling of the main-beam," and " raising it into his place." All this is described in the journal of Bradford with a pathos and a power which could not be surpassed.

I must not detain you either by attempting to portray, in any words of my own, their arrival, on the 21st of November, within the sheltering arm of yonder noble Cape, — "the coast fringed with ice — dreary forests, interspersed with sandy tracts, filling the background; "—" no friendly light-houses, as yet, hanging out their cressets on your headlands; no brave pilot boat hovering like a sea-bird on the tops of the waves, to guide the shattered bark to its harbor; no charts and soundings making the secret pathways of the deep plain as a gravelled road through a lawn." All this was depicted, at the great second-centennial celebration of the settle-ment of Barnstable, by my lamented friend Edward

Everett, with a grandeur of diction and imagery which no living orator can approach. They seem still ringing in my ear from his own lips, — for I was by his side on that occasion, and no one who heard him on that day can ever forget his tones or his words, as, "with a spirit raised above mere natural agencies," he exclaimed, — "I see the mountains of New England rising from their rocky thrones. They rush forward into the ocean, settling down as they advance, and there they range themselves, a mighty bulwark around the heaven-directed vessel. Yes, the everlasting God himself stretches out the arm of his mercy and his power in substantial manifestation, and gathers the meek company of his worshippers as in the hollow of his hand!"

Nor will I detain you for a moment on the simple but solemn covenant which the Pilgrim Fathers formed and signed in the cabin of the Mayflower on that same 21st of November, — the earliest "original compact" of self-government of which we have any authentic record in the annals of our race. That has had ample illustration on many other occasions, and has just been the subject of special commemoration by the New England Historic-Genealogical Society in Boston.

I turn at once to what concerns this day and this hour. I turn at once to that third exploring party which left the Mayflower — not quite blown up by the rashness of a mischievous boy, and still riding at anchor in Cape Cod harbor — on the 16th of December; and for whose wanderings in search of a final place of settlement our friend Dr. Dexter has supplied so precise a chronological table. I turn to those " ten of our men," with " two of our seamen," and with six of the ship's company, — eighteen in all, — in an open shallop, who, after spending a large part of two days " in getting clear of a sandy point, which lay within less than a furlong of the ship," — "the weather being very cold and hard," two of their number " very sick " and one of them almost " swooning with the cold," and the gunner for a day and a night seemingly " sick unto death," — found "smoother water and better sailing" on the 17th, but " so cold that the water froze on their clothes and made them many times like coats of iron;" who were startled at midnight by "a great and hideous cry," and after a fearful but triumphant " first encounter," early the next morning, with a band of Indians, who assailed them with savage yells and showers of arrows, and after a hardly less fearful encounter with a furious storm, which " split their mast in three pieces," and swept them so far upon the breakers that the cry was suddenly heard from the helmsman, " About with her, or else we are all cast away," found themselves at last, when the darkness of midnight had almost overtaken them, " under the lee of a small island, and remained all that night in safety," " keeping their watch in the rain."

- 7

There they passed the 19th, exploring the island. and perhaps repairing their shattered mast. The record is brief but suggestive: "Here we made our rendezvous all that day, being Saturday." But briefer still, and how much more suggestive and significant. is the entry of the following day! —

" 10. (20) of December. on the Sabboth day wee rested."

I pause, — I pause for a moment. — at that most impressive record. Among all the marvellous concisenesses and tersenesses of a Thucydides or a Tacitus, — condensing a whole chapter of philosophy, or the whole character of an individual or a people. into the compass of a motto. — I know of nothing terser or more condensed than this: nor any thing which develops and expands. as we ponder it. into a fuller or finer or more characteristic picture of those whom it describes. "On the Sabbath day we rested." It was no mere secular or physical rest. The day before had sufficed for that. But alone. upon a desert island, in the depths of a stormy winter: wellnigh without food, wholly without shelter; after a week of such experiences. such exposure and hardship and suffering. that the bare recital at this hour almost freezes our blood; without an idea that the morrow should be other or better than the day before; with every conceivable motive. on their own account. and on account of those whom they had left in the ship. to lose not an instant of time, but

to hasten and hurry forward to the completion of
the work of exploration which they had undertaken,
— they still "remembered the Sabbath day to keep
it holy." "On the Sabbath day we rested."

It does not require one to sympathize with the
extreme Sabbatarian strictness of Pilgrim or Puritan, in order to be touched by the beauty of such
a record and of such an example. I know of no
monument on the face of the earth, ancient or
modern, which would appeal more forcibly to the
hearts of all who reverence an implicit and heroic
obedience to the commandments of God, than would
an unadorned stone on yonder Clark's island, with
the simple inscription, "20 Dec. 1620 — On the
Sabbath day we rested." There is none to which
I would myself more eagerly contribute. But it
should be paid for by the penny contributions of
the Sabbath-school children of all denominations
throughout the land, among whom that beautiful
Jubilee Medal has just been distributed.

And what added interest is given to that record,
what added force to that example, by the immediate
sequel! The record of the very next day runs, —
"On Monday we sounded the harbour and found it
a very good harbour for our shipping; we marched
also into the land, and found divers corn-fields and
little running brooks, a place very good for situation;
so we returned to our ship again with good news to
the rest of our people, which did much comfort
their hearts."

That was the day, my friends, which we are here
to commemorate. On that Monday, the 21st of
December, 1620, from a single shallop, those "ten
of our men," with "two of our seamen," and with
six of the ship's company, landed upon this shore.
The names of almost all of them are given, and
should not fail of audible mention on an occasion
like this. Miles Standish heads the roll. John
Carver comes second. Then follow William Bradford, Edward Winslow, John Tilley, Edward Tilley,
John Howland, Richard Warren, Steven Hopkins,
and Edward Dotey. The "two of our seamen"
were John Alderton and Thomas English; and the
two of the ship's company whose names are recorded
were Master Copin and Master Clarke, from the
latter of whom the Sabbath island was called.

They have landed. They have landed at last,
after sixty-six days of weary and perilous naviga-
tion since bidding a final farewell to the receding
shores of their dear native country. They have
landed at last; and when the sun of that day went
down, after the briefest circuit of the year, New
England had a place and a name — a permanent
place, a never to be obliterated name — in the history, as well as in the geography, of civilized
Christian man.

> " They whom once the desert beach
> Pent within its bleak domain, —
> Soon their ample sway shall stretch
> O'er the plenty of the plain ! "

I will not say that the corner-stone of New England had quite yet been laid. But its symbol and perpetual synonyme had certainly been found. That one grand Rock, — even then without its fellow along the shore, and destined to be without its fellow on any shore throughout the world, — Nature had laid it, — The Architect of the Universe had laid it, — "when the morning stars sang together, and all the sons of God shouted for joy." There it had reposed, unseen of human eye, the storms and floods of centuries beating and breaking upon it. There it had reposed, awaiting the slow-coming feet, which, guided and guarded by no mere human power, were now to make it famous for ever. The Pilgrims trod it, as it would seem, unconsciously, and left nothing but authentic tradition to identify it. "Their rock was not as our rock." Their thoughts at that hour were upon no stone of earthly mould. If they observed at all what was beneath their feet, it may indeed have helped them still more fervently to lift their eyes to Him who had been predicted and promised " as the shadow of a great rock in a weary land;" and may have given renewed emphasis to the psalm which perchance they may have recalled, — " From the end of the earth will I cry unto thee, when my heart is overwhelmed: lead me to the rock that is higher than I." Their trust was only on the Rock of Ages.

We have had many glowing descriptions and not

a few elaborate pictures of this day's doings; and it has sometimes been a matter of contention whether Mary Chilton or John Alden first leapt upon the shore, — a question which the late Judge Davis proposed to settle by humorously suggesting that the friends of John Alden should give place to the lady, as a matter of gallantry. But the Mayflower, with John Alden, and Mary Chilton, and all the rest of her sex, and all the children, was still in the harbor of Cape Cod. The aged Brewster, also, was on board the Mayflower with them; and sorely needed must his presence and consolation have been, as poor Bradford returned to the ship, after a week's absence, to find that his wife had fallen overboard and was drowned the very day after his departure.

I may not dwell on these or any other details, except to recall the fact that on Friday, the 25th, they weighed anchor, — it was Christmas Day, though they did not recognize it, as so many of us are just preparing to recognize it, as the brightest and best of all the days of the year; — that on Saturday, the 26th, the Mayflower "came safely into a safe harbour;" and that on Monday, the 28th, the landing was completed. Not only was the time come and the place found, but the whole company of those who were for ever to be associated with that time and that place were gathered at last where we are now gathered to do homage to their memory.

I make no apology, sons and daughters of New

England, for having kept always in the foreground
of the picture I have attempted to draw, the religious aspects and incidents of the event we have
come to commemorate. Whatever civil or political
accompaniments or consequences that event may
have had, it was in its rise and progress, in its incep-
tion and completion, eminently and exclusively a
religious movement. The Pilgrims left Scrooby as
a church. They settled in Amsterdam and in
Leyden as a church. They embarked in the Mayflower as a church. They came to New England
as a church; and Morton, at the close of the introduction to Bradford's History, as given by Dr. Young
in his Chronicles, entitles it " The Church of Christ
at Plymouth in New England, first begun in Old
England, and carried on in Holland and Plymouth
aforesaid." They had no license, indeed, from
either Pope or Primate. It was a church not only
without a bishop, but without even a pastor; with
only a layman to lead their devotions and administer
their discipline. A grand layman he was, — Elder
Brewster: it would be well for the world if there
were more laymen like him, at home and abroad.
In yonder Bay, it is true, before setting foot on Cape
Cod, they entered into a compact of civil government; but the reason expressly assigned for so doing
was, that "some of the strangers amongst them
(*i. e.*, not Leyden men, but adventurers who joined
them in England) had let fall in the ship that when

they came ashore they would use their own liberty,
for none had power to command them," or, as elsewhere stated, because they had observed "some not
well affected to unity and concord, but gave some
appearance of faction." They came as a Church: all
else was incidental, the result of circumstances, a
protection against outsiders. They came to secure
a place to worship God according to the dictates of
their own consciences, free from the molestations
and persecutions which they had encountered in
England; and free, too, from the uncongenial surroundings, the irregular habits of life, the strange
and uncouth language, the licentiousness of youth,
the manifold temptations, and "the neglect of obser-
vation of the Lord's day as a Sabbath," which they
had so lamented in Holland.

We cannot be too often reminded that it was
religion which effected the first permanent settlement in New England. All other motives had
failed. Commerce, the fisheries, the hope of dis-
covering mines, the ambition of founding Colonies,
all had been tried, and all had failed. But the Pilgrims asked of God; and "He gave them the
heathen for their inheritance, and the uttermost
parts of the earth for their possession." Religious
faith and fear, religious hope and trust, — the fear
of God, the love of Christ, an assured faith in the
Holy Scriptures, and an assured hope of a life of
bliss and blessedness to come, — these, and these

alone, proved sufficient to animate and strengthen them for the endurance of all the toils and trials which such an enterprise involved. Let it never be forgotten that if the corner-stone of New England was indeed laid by the Pilgrim Fathers, two centuries and a half ago to-day, it was in the cause of religion they laid it; and whatever others may have built upon it since, or may build upon it hereafter, — " gold, silver, precious stones, wood, hay, stubble," — God forbid that on this Anniversary the foundation should be ignored or repudiated!

As we look back ever so cursorily on the great procession of American History as it starts from yonder Rock, and winds on and on and on to the present hour, we may descry many other scenes, many other actors, remote and recent, in other parts of the Union as well as in our own, of the highest interest and importance. There are Conant and Endicott with their little rudimental plantations at Cape Ann and at Salem. There is the elder Winthrop, with the Massachusetts Charter, at Boston, of whom the latest and best of New England Historians (Dr. Palfrey) has said " that it was his policy, more than any other man's, that organized into shape, animated with practical vigor, and prepared for permanency, those primeval sentiments and institutions that have directed the course of thought and action in New England in later times." There is the younger Winthrop, not far behind, with the Charter of Connecticut, of whose separate Colonies Hooker and Haynes and Hopkins and Eaton and Davenport and Ludlow had laid the foundations. There is Roger Williams, "the Apostle of soul freedom," as he has been called, with the Charter of Rhode Island. There is the brave and generous Stuyvesant of the New Netherlands. There are the Catholic Calverts, and the noble Quaker Penn, building up Maryland and Pennsylvania alike, upon principles of toleration and philanthropy. There is the benevolent and chivalrous Oglethorpe, assisted by Whitefield and the sainted Wesleys, planting his Moravian Colony in Georgia. There is Franklin, with his first proposal of a Continental Union, and with his countless inventions in political as well as physical science. There is James Otis with his great argument against Writs of Assistance, and Samuel Adams with his inexorable demand for the removal of the British regiments from Boston. There are Quincy with his grand remonstrance against the Port Bill, and Warren, offering himself as the Proto-martyr on Bunker Hill. There is Jefferson with the Declaration of Independence fresh from his own pen, with John Adams close at his side, as its "Colossus on the floor of Congress." There are Hamilton and Madison and Jay bringing forward the Constitution in their united arms; and there, leaning on their shoulders, and on that Constitution, but towering above them all, is WASHINGTON, the consummate commander, the incomparable President, the world-honored Patriot. There are Marshall and Story as the expounders of the Constitution, and Webster as its defender. There is John Quincy Adams with his powerful and persistent plea for the sacred Right of Petition. There is Jackson with his Proclamation against Nullification. There is Lincoln with his ever memorable Proclamation of Emancipation. And there, closing for the moment that procession of the dead, — for I presume not to marshal the living, — is George Peabody, with his world-wide munificence and his countless benefactions. Other figures may present themselves to other eyes as that grand Panorama is unrolled. Other figures will come into view as that great procession advances. But be it prolonged, as we pray God it may be, even " to the crack of doom," first and foremost, as it moves on and on in radiant files, — " searing the eyeballs " of oppressors and tyrants, but rejoicing the hearts of the lovers of freedom throughout the world, — will ever be seen and recognized the men whom we commemorate to-day, — the Pilgrim Fathers of New England. No herald announces their approach. No pomp or parade attends their advent. "Shielded and helmed and weapon'd with the truth," no visible guards are around them, either for honor or defence. Bravely but humbly, and almost unconsciously, they assume their perilous posts, as pioneers of an advance which is to know no backward steps, until, throughout this Western hemisphere, it shall have prepared the way of the Lord and of liberty. They come with no charter of human inspiration. They come with nothing but the open Bible in their hands, leading a march of civilization and human freedom, which shall go on until time shall be no more, — if only that Bible shall remain open, and shall be accepted and reverenced, by their descendants as it was by themselves, as the Word of God!

It is a striking coincidence that while they were just taking the first steps in the movement which terminated at Plymouth Rock, that great clerical Commission was appointed by King James, which prepared what has everywhere been received as the standard English version of the Holy Scriptures; and which, though they continued to use the Geneva Bible themselves, has secured to their children and posterity a translation which is the choicest treasure of literature as well as of religion. Nor can I fail to remember, with the warmest interest, that, at this moment, while we are engaged in this Fifth Jubilee Commemoration, a similar Commission is employed, for the first time, in subjecting that translation to the most critical revision; — not with a view, certainly, to attempt any change or improvement of its incomparable style and language, but only to purge the sacred volume from every human interpolation or error.

No more beautiful scene has been witnessed in our day and generation, nor one more auspicious of that Christian unity which another world shall witness, if not this, than the scene presented in Westminster Abbey, in the exquisite chapel of Henry VII., by that Revision Commission, in immediate preparation for entering on their great task, on the morning of the 22d of June last; — " such a scene," as the accomplished Dean Alford has well said, " as has not been enacted since the name of Christ was first named in Britain." I can use no other words than his, in describing it: " Between the latticed shrine of King Henry VII. and the flat pavement tomb of Edward VI. was spread ' God's board,' and round that pavement tomb knelt, shoulder to shoulder, bishops and dignitaries of the Church of England, professors of her Universities, divines of the Scottish Presbyterian and Free Churches, and of the Independent, Baptist, Wesleyan, Unitarian Churches in England, — a representative assembly, such as our Church has never before gathered under her wing, of the Catholic Church by her own definition, — of ' all who profess and call themselves Christians.' " It was a scene to give character to an age; and should the commission produce no other valuable fruit, that opening Communion will make it memorable to the end of time.

Yes, the open Bible was the one and all-sufficient

support and reliance of the Pilgrim Fathers. They looked, indeed, for other and greater reformations in religion than any which Luther or Calvin had accomplished or advocated; but they looked for them to come from a better understanding and a more careful study of the Holy Scriptures, and not from any vainglorious human wisdom or scientific investigations. As their pastor Robinson said, in his farewell discourse, " He was confident the Lord had more truth and light yet to break forth out of his Holy Word."

Let me not seem, my friends, to exaggerate the importance to our country of the event which we this day celebrate. The Pilgrims of the Mayflower did not establish the earliest permanent English settlement within the territories which now constitute our beloved country. I would by no means overlook or disparage the prior settlement at Jamestown in Virginia. The Old Dominion, with all its direct and indirect associations with Sir Walter Raleigh, and with Shakspeare's accomplished patron and friend, the Earl of Southampton, — with Pocahontas, too, and Captain John Smith, — must always be remembered by the old Colony with the respect and affection due to an elder sister. "I said an elder, not a better." Yet we may well envy some of her claims to distinction. More than ten years before an English foot had planted itself on the soil of New England, that Virginia Colony had effected a settlement ; and more than a year before the landing of the Pilgrims, — on the 30th of July, 1619, — the first Representative Legislative Assembly ever held within the limits of the United States was convened at Jamestown. That Assembly passed a significant Act against drunkenness; and an Act somewhat quaint in its terms and provisions, but whose influence might not be unwholesome at this day, against " excessive apparel," — providing that every man should be assessed in the church for all public contributions, " if he be unmarried, according to his own apparel; if he be married, according to his own and his wife's, or either of their apparel." Such a statute would have been called puritanical, if it had emanated from a New England Legislature. It might even now, however, do something to diminish the dimensions, and simplify the material, and abate the luxurious extravagance, of modern dress. But that first Jamestown Assembly passed another most noble Act, for the conversion of the Indians and the education of their children, which entitles Virginia to claim pre-eminence, or certainly priority, in that great work of Christian philanthropy, for which our Fathers, with glorious John Eliot at their head, did so much, and for which their sons, alas! have accomplished so little, — unless, perhaps, under the new and noble Indian policy of the last twelve months. The political organization of Virginia was almost mature, while that of New England was still in embryo.

Again, I do not forget that the Pilgrims of the Mayflower built up no great City or Commonwealth. Within the first three months after their landing, one-half of their number had fallen victims to the rigors of the climate and the hardships of their condition; and at the end of ten years the whole population of the Colony — men, women, and children — did not exceed three hundred. They were but as a voice in the desert; but it was a glorious voice, and one which was destined to reverberate around the world, and ring along the ages with still increasing emphasis. Other Colonies, by the inspiration and encouragement of their example, soon succeeded them, and did the substantial work for which they only prepared the way; for which they, as they said themselves, were but "stepping-stones." The great "Suffolk Emigration" of 1630, — "The Governor and Company of the Massachusetts Bay," — coming over in eleven ships, with the whole government and its Charter, were the main founders and builders of the grand old Commonwealth, of which the Plymouth Colony, sixty years afterwards, became an honored part.

It is pleasant to remember how harmoniously and lovingly the two Colonies lived together. It is pleasant to remember that parting charge of John Cotton to the Massachusetts Company, at Southampton, "that they should take advice of them at Plymouth, and do nothing to offend them." I cannot forget, either, the cordial visit of Governor Bradford to Governor Winthrop in 1631; nor that Winthrop soon afterwards subjected himself to reproach for supplying the Pilgrims with powder, at his personal cost, in a moment of their urgent danger and distress. Still less can I forget that October day in 1632, when Governor Winthrop returned Bradford's visit, coming a large part of the way here on foot, and crossing the river on the back of his guide; and when Bradford and Brewster and Roger Williams and Winthrop, with John Wilson, the first pastor of Boston, were together on this spot, engaging in religious discourse, and partaking of the Sacrament together. That most impressive and memorable Communion was at once the harbinger and the pledge, the prediction and the assurance, of the peace and harmony, the co-operation and concord, which were long to prevail between the infant Colonies of New England.

True, there were some shades of difference in the religious sentiment and in the civil administration of the various plantations, as they were successively developed. The charges of intolerance, bigotry, superstition, and persecution, which there seems to have been a special delight, in some quarters, of late years, in arraying against our New England Fathers and founders, apply without doubt more directly to other Colonies, than to that whose landing we this day commemorate. The Pilgrims in their narrow retreat of rock and sand were but little disturbed by "intruders and dissentients," — as my friend Dr. Ellis has so well classified them, — and could afford to be less rigid in their admissions and exclusions. Their leaders, too, were perhaps of a somewhat more lenient and liberal temper than those who settled elsewhere. Let them have all the honor which belongs to them; and let censure and condemnation fall wherever it is deserved! I am not here to justify or excuse all the extravagances, superstitions, or persecutions of the Puritan Colonists. But still less am I here to pander to the prurient malignity of those who are never weary of prying into the petty faults and follies of our Fathers, and who seem to gloat and exult in holding them up to the ridicule and reproach of their children. As if those great hearts, whether of 1620 or 1630, had fled into the wilderness to assert and vindicate a broad, abstract, unqualified doctrine of religious liberty, or even of religious toleration, to which they had afterwards proved recreant themselves! As if the precarious circumstances of their condition — with savage foes watching to extirpate them, with famine ever staring them in the face, with disease and death menacing them in every shape and at every turn — did not constrain and compel them, in the earlier stages of their career, to adopt the principle of excluding from their community any and all who were bent upon introducing contention and discord, and of enforcing among themselves something of that stern martial rule which belongs to a besieged camp! Why, even Roger Williams himself was forced to introduce a right of exclusion, or non-admission, into his original articles of settlement at Providence. We can never too often recall the language of the late venerable Josiah Quincy, — the last man of our day and generation — I had almost said of any day and generation — to palliate real bigotry or wanton intolerance, — when he said, in his masterly Discourse on the Second Centennial Anniversary of the Settlement of Boston in 1630 : " Had our early ancestors adopted the course we at this day are apt to deem so easy and obvious, and placed their government on the basis of liberty for all sorts of consciences, it would have been, in that age, a certain introduction of anarchy. . . . The non-toleration which characterized our early ancestors, from whatever source it may have originated, had undoubtedly the effect they intended and wished. It excluded from influence, in their infant settlement, all the friends and adherents of the ancient monarchy and hierarchy; all who, from any motive, ecclesiastical or civil, were disposed to disturb their peace or their churches. They considered it

a measure of 'self-defence.' And it is unquestion-
able that it was chiefly instrumental in forming the
homogeneous and exclusively republican character
for which the people of New England have, in all
times, been distinguished; and, above all, that it
fixed irrevocably in the country that noble security
for religious liberty, the independent system of
Church Government."

But whatever may have been the differences or
disagreements of the first planters of Plymouth and
Massachusetts Bay, of New Haven and of Connecticut, at the outset, we all know that in the
summer of 1643 these four original Colonies established that noble New England Confederation, — the
model and prototype of the Confederation of 1778,
which "blended the many-nationed whole in one,"
and carried the thirteen American Colonies through
the War of Independence, — whose grand and
comprehensive preamble is alone an ample reply
to all who would magnify one Colony at the ex-
pense of another: —

"Whereas we all came into these parts of America with one and the same end and aim, namely, to
advance the Kingdom of our Lord Jesus Christ and
to enjoy the liberties of the Gospel in purity with
peace: And whereas in our settling (by a wise
providence of God) we are further dispersed upon
the Seacoasts and Rivers than was at first intended,
so that we cannot according to our desire with

convenience communicate in one Government and Jurisdiction: And whereas we live encompassed with people of several Nations and strange languages, which hereafter may prove injurious to us or our posterity: And forasmuch as the Natives have formerly committed sundry insolences and outrages upon several plantations of the English, and have of late combined themselves against us: And seeing by reason of those sad distractions in England which they have heard of, and by which they know we are hindered from that humble way of seeking advice, or reaping those comfortable fruits of protection which at other times we might well expect: We therefore do conceive it our bounden duty without delay to enter into a present Consociation amongst ourselves, for mutual help and strength in all our future concernments: That as in Nation and Religion so in other respects we be and continue ONE, according to the tenor and true meaning of the ensuing Articles: Wherefore it is fully agreed and concluded by and between the parties or Jurisdictions above-named, and they jointly and severally do by these presents agree and conclude, That they all be and henceforth be called by the name of The United Colonies of New England."

The very next clause of this remarkable Ordinance provided as follows: " The said United Colonies for themselves and their posterities do jointly and severally hereby enter into a firm and perpetual league of friendship and amity for offence and defence, mutual advice and succour, upon all just occasions both for preserving and propagating the truth and liberties of the Gospel and for their own mutual safety and welfare." And another article provided for intrusting the whole management of the Confederation to two Commissioners from each of the four Jurisdictions, carefully adding, "all in Church fellowship with us," — thus leaving no shadow of doubt upon the point that it was a "Consociation" for religious as well as for political peace and unity.

Accordingly we find among the proceedings of the Commissioners at New Haven in 1646 — a meeting at which neither Bradford nor Winslow nor either of the Winthrops was present, but at which all of the four Colonies were fully represented, and to whose proceedings all of them ultimately subscribed — that most memorable Declaration as to the "Spreading nature of Error and the dangerous growth and effects thereof," "under a deceitful colour of liberty of conscience," which recommended, among other things, that "Anabaptism, Familism, Antinomianism, and generally all errours of a like nature," "be seasonably and duly suppressed;" and which concluded with that glowing prediction for New England: "If thus we be for God, he will certainly be with us; and though the God of the world (as he is styled) be worshipped, and by usurpation set upon his throne in the main and greatest part of America, yet this small part and portion may be vindicated as by the right hand of Jehovah, and justly called Emmanuel's land."

I do not forget that, in reference to the clause recommending the suppression of errors, the Plymouth Commissioners "desired further consideration;" but the whole Declaration is entered upon the Plymouth Records as agreed upon, and was ultimately subscribed alike by the Commissioners of all the Colonies.

I do not forget, either, that all New England was not included in that Confederation. All that there was of New Hampshire was indeed within the jurisdiction of Massachusetts. But we miss Rhode Island from the historic group. We miss Clarke and Coddington and Roger Williams from the roll of the Commissioners. It must be borne in mind, however, that it was not because the Plantations at Providence and the Islands were opposed to the Confederation or any of its articles, that they were not members of it. Both of them desired and solicited admission. "There was yet another, a fifth New England Colony (said John Quincy Adams in 1843), denied admission into the Union, and furnishing, in its broadest latitude, the demonstration of that conscientious, contentious spirit, which so signally characterized the English Puritans of the seventeenth century, the founders of New England, of all the liberties of the British Nation, and of the ultimate universal freedom of the race of man. The founder of the Colony of Rhode Island (adds he) was Roger Williams, a man who may be considered the very impersonation of this combined conscientious, contentious spirit."

Rhode Island may well afford to bear with equanimity any charges against the early contentiousness of her founders, in view of the glory which that very contentiousness has acquired for her on the page of history. "Roger Williams (says Bancroft) was the first person in modern Christendom to assert in its plenitude the doctrine of the liberty of conscience, the equality of opinions before the law; and in its defence he was the harbinger of Milton, the precursor and superior of Jeremy Taylor." The man upon whose tombstone such an inscription, — even with some allowances for rhetorical exaggeration, — may be justly written, need fear no strictures to which other peculiarities of character or conduct may subject him. I have an hereditary disposition, too, to be not only just but tender towards his memory, for Williams and the Winthrops of old, in spite of all differences, were most loving friends from first to last. I would palliate not a particle of the persecution or cruelty which he suffered; from whatever source it may have proceeded, or by whomever it may have been prompted. There was an heroic grandeur in his endurance and fortitude; there was an unsparing self-devotion in his care for the Indians; there was a simplicity, sincerity, and earnestness in his whole career and character,— which must ever command our warmest sympathy and admiration.

But it would be gross injustice to our other New England Fathers, and especially to our Massachusetts Fathers, not to admit that the conduct of Williams, in some of its earlier manifestations, was too precipitate and turbulent to be compatible with the peace and safety of the infant Colonies, — denying, as Winslow says he did, the lawfulness of a public oath, refusing "to allow the colors of our nation," and holding forth the unlawfulness of the patent from the king; — while the condition and temper of the plantations of Rhode Island — a State which we now so honor and love, and to which we owe more than one of our most valued citizens — were such, at that time, as to cause even the Plymouth rulers and elders to say: "Concerning the Islanders, we have no conversing with them, nor desire to have, further than necessity or humanity may require."

But with the exception of these Rhode Island Plantations, which were still very small and scattered, New England was then one; one, not only as the multiplied States of our American Union are one at this day, for civil, political, and military purposes; but one, also, in a unity to which our Federal Constitution presents no counterpart; — one for the preservation and propagation of Religion; a Union for the defence and diffusion of pure, Protestant Christianity, such as the world had hardly ever witnessed before, and may hardly ever witness again. It was a grand Experiment, conceived and instituted for the glory of God and the welfare of man's estate. But a higher than human power had long ago emphatically declared, "My Kingdom is not of this world;" and the result gave abundant evidence that, on this Continent at least, the Temporal and Spiritual power were not destined to be wielded successfully by the same hands. Church and State were never meant to thrive together on American soil. It remains to be seen how long they are to thrive together anywhere.

I hasten to the conclusion of this discourse. I may not attempt to pursue the thread of Pilgrim history further on this occasion. We all know what New England has been doing since the days of that Confederation. We all know how her sons and her daughters, besides founding and building up noble institutions within her own limits, have sought homes in other parts of the country, near and remote, and how powerfully their influence and enterprise have everywhere been felt. It may safely be said that there is hardly a State, or county, or town, or village, on the Continent, in which New England men and women are not turning their faces towards Plymouth Rock to-day with something of the affectionate yearning of children towards an ancestral, or even a parental, home. We all know what contributions they have made to the cause of Education, of Learning, of Literature, of Science, and of Art. We all know what they have done for Commerce on the ocean, and for Industry on the land, vexing every sea with their keels, and startling every waterfall with their looms. We all know what examples of Patriotism and Statesmanship they have exhibited in every hour of Colonial or National trial. We do not fail to remember that New England led the march to Independence at Lexington and Concord and Bunker Hill, and that the bones of her sons were mingled with almost every soil on which the battles of the Revolution were fought. Still less can we forget with what alacrity and heroic self-sacrifice her bravest and best rushed forth, — so many of them, alas! never to return, — for the defence of the Union, in the great struggle which has so recently terminated.

But we are not here to-day to boast of our own exploits, or to deal with the events of our own day. It becomes us rather to remember our own short-comings and our own unworthiness, in view of the

sublime examples of piety, endurance, and heroic
valor which were exhibited by those "holy and
humble men of heart" by whom our Colonies were
planted. We sometimes assume to sit in judgment
upon their doings. We often criticise their faults
and failings. There is a special proneness of late
years to deride their superstitions and denounce
their intolerance. And certainly we may well
rejoice that the days of religious bigotry and pro-
scription are over in our land. But is it not even
more true at this hour, than when no less liberal a
Christian than John Quincy Adams uttered the
warning, thirty years ago, that the intensely religious
feelings and prejudices of our infancy have not only
given way to universal toleration, but "to a liberality
of doctrine bordering upon the extreme of a faltering faith"? God forbid that our own religious
freedom should ever be described as Gibbon
described that of the age of Antoninus, from which
he dates the decline and fall of the Roman Empire:
"The various modes of worship (says he) which
prevailed in the Roman world were all considered
by the people as equally true; by the philosophers
as equally false; and by the magistrates as equally
useful. And thus toleration produced not only
mutual indulgence, but even religious concord."
Such a spirit of toleration, — such religious liberty
as that, — even in an age of Paganism, gradually led
to the overthrow of the great Empire of the Old

World. What else but overthrow can it accomplish in a Christian age for the great Republic of the New World?

May it not be wise and well for us all sometimes to reflect — and may I not be pardoned for concluding this discourse by summoning the sons and daughters of New England, here and everywhere, to reflect this day — what judgment would be pronounced upon us by our Pilgrim and our Puritan Fathers, could they be permitted to behold and to comprehend the grand expansion and development which we now witness of the institutions which they planted? Could they descend among us, at this moment, in bodily presence, and with organs capable of embracing at a glance a full perception and understanding of every thing which has been accomplished on this wide-spread continent, since they were withdrawn from these earthly scenes and entered into their rest, — what would they think, what would they say?

It is not difficult to imagine the surprise with which they would contemplate the existing condition of New England, and of the mighty nation of which it forms a part. It is not difficult to imagine the astonishment with which they would regard the great inventions and improvements of modern times. It is not difficult to imagine the eager and incredulous amazement with which Miles Standish, for instance, would listen to the click of a little machine, almost at his own old doorway, which could supply him daily and hourly with the latest phases of the big wars in Europe, which in his lifetime he could only have studied in bulletins, or broadsides, or "books of the news," not much less than half a year old. It is not difficult to conceive the wonder of Edward Winslow, as he should see, or be told of, some noble ship traversing the wide Atlantic, from Land's End to Cape Cod, with undeviating regularity, without sails and against the wind, in far less time than he could have relied on crossing from one little island to another of the Caribbean Sea, before he sunk so sadly beneath its waters. It is not difficult to picture the bewilderment of Brewster and Bradford as they should listen to the rattling and whistling and thundering, by day and by night, of cars bringing more passengers than the whole population of Plymouth in their day, and more freight than would have sustained that whole population for a winter, not merely from Boston in not much more than an hour, but from the shores of the Pacific Ocean in not much more than a week! It is easy to conceive the consternation of them all, could they see this whole assembly, by an almost instantaneous flash of sunlight, grouped and pictured with an exactness which the most protracted labors of ancient or modern art could never have reached. It is easy to conceive their rapture should they witness the intensest physical agonies of the human frame charmed to sleep by the inhalation of the vapor of a few drops of ether. It is easy to understand how astounded they would be, not merely at learning that all those phenomena of the celestial bodies which had so often perplexed and alarmed them were now familiar to every school-boy; but at being specially informed that to-morrow there should be a great eclipse of the sun, total in some parts of the world though hardly visible here; and that Science, not satisfied with calculating, by the old processes of which they may have heard something before, the precise instants of its beginning and end, had equipped and sent out formal expeditions to many distant lands to observe and record all its phases and incidents!

We can readily suppose that such marvels as these would not be taken in by them without reawakening something of their old superstitious fear and awe; and we might expect to hear from their lips some exclamations, if not about "the old Serpent," certainly about " wonders and more wonders of the invisible world." But we need not resort to these miracles of science and art in order to illustrate the surprise and amazement with which our Fathers would contemplate the condition of their posterity. The mere extent, population, and power of our country, its great States, its magnificent cities, its vast wealth, its commerce, its crops, its industry, its education, its freedom, — no longer a slave upon its soil, — all, all of all races, equal before the law, — what else could they desire to fill up the measure of our development, or of their own delight! What more could they possibly wish to complete and crown the vision of glory vouchsafed to them?

Oh, my friends, have you forgotten, or can you imagine that they would forget for an instant, the cause in which they came here? Can you believe that they would be so dazzled and blinded by the glare of mere temporal success and material prosperity, or by the grandeur of intellectual triumphs and scientific discoveries and philosophical achievements, as to lose sight and thought of that which animated — and, I had almost said, constituted — their whole mortal existence? Can we not hear them inquiring eagerly and earnestly, as they gaze upon all around them, "Is the moral welfare of the country keeping pace with its material progress? Has religion maintained the place we assigned it, as the corner-stone of all your institutions? Is the Bible, the open Bible, which we brought over in our hands, still reverenced of you all as the Word of God? Is the Lord's Day still respected and observed as a day of religious rest, as we observed it on that desolate island before our feet had stept upon yonder consecrated rock? Are your houses of worship proportionate to your population? Are there worshippers enough, Sunday by Sunday, to fill the houses which you have? Are there no temples of false prophets — no organized communities of licentiousness, under the color of religion — in your land? Are there none among you who 'seek unto them that have familiar spirits and unto wizards that peep and that, mutter, — for the living to the dead'? Are you doing your full part in carrying the Gospel to the heathen? Or are you waiting until the heathen shall have come over into your inheritance, bringing their idols with them, to cheapen labor and to dilute your own civilization and Christianity? Are your schools and colleges still dedicated, as we dedicated at least one of them, 'to Christ and the Church'? Is there no fear that your science has been emboldened by its triumphant successes to overleap the bounds of legitimate investigation, putting Nature to the rack to wring from her, if it were possible, some denial, or some doubt, of that great Original, whom she has always rejoiced, and still rejoices, to proclaim? Is there no fear that your philosophy has been tempted to transcend the just 'limits of religious thought,' and to set up some material theory, or some self-styled positive system, which may seduce the deluded soul from its hope of immortality, and weaken, if not destroy, its sense of the need of a Saviour? Is there no fear that a sentimental, sensational, licentious literature is corrupting the tastes and sapping the morals of your children, and rendering the universal appetite for reading an almost doubtful blessing? Are your charities, public and private, numerous and noble as they are, altogether commensurate with your wealth? Or is the larger half of your surplus incomes absorbed in a cankering and debasing luxury, destructive alike to the physical, intellectual, and spiritual energy of all who indulge in it? Are integrity and virtue enthroned in your hearts and homes? Have they a recognized and undisputed sovereignty in the market-place and on the exchange? Or are vice and crime making not a few days dark, and not a few nights hideous, in your crowded cities? Is there purity and principle and honor in your public servants? Or are corruption and intrigue and fraud threatening to make havoc of your free institutions, rendering all things venal, and almost all things, except mere party disloyalty, venial, in your State and National Capitals?"

Such questions as these, I am conscious, if coming from any living lips, or, certainly, from any living layman's lips, might be jeered at as savoring of sanctimoniousness and fanaticism. I do not presume to ask them for myself; much less would I presume to answer them. Make what allowance you please for the rigid austerity and excessive scrupulousness of those for whom I am only an interpreter. But does any one deny or doubt that they are the very questions which would be asked first, and most eagerly and most emphatically, by those whom we this day commemorate, and by those who were associated with them in founding and building up New England?

Can we not hear them, at this moment, solemnly warning us, lest, in the pride of our prosperity and greatness, " when our silver and our gold is multiplied, and all that we have is multiplied," our hearts be lifted up to say, each for himself, " My power and the might of mine hand hath gotten me this wealth," while the great lesson of our stewardship, to Him to whom we owe it all, is forgotten or neglected?

Can we not hear them, at this moment, solemnly warning us, lest, in the pride of our freedom and independence, we forget that " the liberty we are to stand for, with the hazard not only of our goods, but of our lives if need be," is " a liberty for that only which is good, just, and honest," and not a liberty to be used as a cloak of maliciousness and licentiousness?

Can we not hear them, at this moment, from yonder hill of graves, solemnly and affectionately warning us lest, in the pride of our science, while a thousand telescopes and spectroscopes are ready to be levelled, on the morrow, at the orb of day, — to reveal its chromosphere and its photosphere, to measure its tornadoes, to detect the exact nature of its corona, and to mark the precise instants of its

partial or total obscuration, — the Sun of Righteous-
ness, all unobserved, be dimmed and darkened in
our own hearts, and an Eclipse of Faith be suffered
to steal and settle over our land, whose beginning
may be imperceptible, and its end beyond calcula-
tion?

Oh, let us hear and heed these warnings of the
fathers to the children, as they come to us to-day,
enforced not only by all the precious memories of
their faith and piety, their virtues and sacrifices and
sufferings, but by all the lessons and experiences
of the times in which we live! We need not look
beyond the events of the single year which is just
closing, — this *Annus Mirabilis*, compared with
which that of Dryden and Defoe was without sig-
nificance or consequence; a year, more marvellous
in its manifestations than almost any which has pre-
ceded it since the great year of our Lord, and from
whose calendar no form of physical, political, or
religious convulsion seems to have been wanting
to startle and confound the nations; a year, whose
Christmas, alas! is clouded and saddened by the
continuance, in a land bound to us by memories
not yet obliterated, of a conflict and a carnage
which must fill every Christian heart with horror,
and for the termination of which we would de-
voutly invoke the only Intervention which has not

been, and which cannot be, rejected; — we need not,
I say, look beyond the events of this single jubilee
year of the Landing, to find evidence of the vanity
of all human ambition and the impotence of all
human power, and to see renewed and startling
proof that while

> "A thousand years scarce serve to form a State,
> An hour may lay it in the dust."

Let us not be deaf to the warnings of the Fathers.
Let us not be insensible to the lessons of the hour.
Let us resolve that no National growth or grandeur,
no civil freedom or social prosperity or individual
success, shall ever render us unmindful of those
great principles of piety and virtue which the
Pilgrims inculcated and exemplified. Let us
resolve that whatever else this nation shall be, or
shall fail to be, it shall still and always be a Christian
Nation, in the full comprehensiveness and true sig-
nificance of that glorious term, — its example ever
on the side of Peace and Justice; its eagle, not
only with the shield of Union and Liberty em-
blazoned on its breast, but, like that of many
a lectern of ancient cathedral or modern church,
abroad or at home, ever proudly bearing up the
open Bible on its outspread wings! And then, as
year after year shall roll over our land, as jubilee
shall succeed jubilee, and our children and our

children's children shall gather on this consecrated
spot to celebrate the event which has brought us
here to-day, those grand closing words of Webster
fifty years ago — the only words worthy to sum up
the emotions of an hour like this, and send them
down all sparkling and blazing to the remotest
posterity, — shall be repeated and repeated by
those who shall successively stand where he then
stood, and where I stand now, not with any feeble
expectation or faltering hope only, but with that firm
persuasion, that undoubting confidence, that assured
trust and faith, with which I adopt and repeat
them as the closing words of another Jubilee discourse : —

"Advance, then, ye future generations! We
would hail you, as you rise in your long succession
to fill the places which we now fill, and to taste
the blessings of existence where we are passing,
and soon shall have passed, our own human duration. We bid you welcome to this pleasant land of
the Fathers. We bid you welcome to the healthful
skies and the verdant fields of New England. We
greet your accession to the great inheritance which
we have enjoyed. We welcome you to the blessings of good government and religious liberty. We
welcome you to the treasures of science and the
delights of learning. We welcome you to the
transcendent sweets of domestic life, to the happi-

ness of kindred and parents and children. We welcome you to the immeasurable blessings of rational existence, the immortal hope of Christianity, and the light of everlasting truth!"

NOTE.

(Page 36.)

THE following inscription in the Hall of the Bishop of London's Palace, at Fulham, was copied for me most kindly by my venerable friend Bishop McIlvaine, of Ohio : —

" This Hall, with the adjoining quadrangle, was erected by Bishop Fitzjames in the reign of Henry VII. on the site of buildings of the old Palace as ancient as the Conquest. It was used as the Hall by Bishop Bonner and Bishop Ridley, during the struggles of the Reformation, and retained its original proportions till it was altered by Bishop Sherlock in the reign of George II. Bishop Howley, in the reign of George IV., changed it into a private unconsecrated Chapel. It is now restored to its original purpose on the erection by Bishop Tait of a new Chapel of more suitable dimensions.

"A. D. 1866."

The Palace must have been occupied by Richard Bancroft, during whose intolerant policy the Pilgrims fled to Holland ; as he was Bishop of London for some years before becoming Archbishop of Canterbury. It must, also, have been occupied by Laud, from whose intolerance the Puritans suffered ; as he, after serving as Bishop of St. David's, and of Bath and Wells, was translated to London in 1628, and continued in that See, exercising great influence over the ecclesiastical affairs of the realm, until he succeeded the more liberal Abbot as Primate of all England.

www.ingramcontent.com/pod-product-compliance
Lightning Source LLC
Chambersburg PA
CBHW020309090426
42735CB00009B/1286